MISSING PERSON

Nicholas Hogg was born in Leicester. Twice short-listed for the Eric Gregory Award for young poets, in 2021 he won the Gregory O'Donoghue International Poetry Prize, and in 2023 the Liverpool Poetry Prize. His award-winning short fiction has been broadcast by the BBC, and his novel, *Tokyo Nobody,* is now a Ridley Scott film starring Eric Bana and *Stranger Things*' Sadie Sink. @nicholas_hogg www.nicholashogg.com

ISBN: 978-1-915760-44-9

Cover designed by Aaron Kent and Joseph Kent

Edited and Typeset by Aaron Kent

Broken Sleep Books Ltd
Rhydwen
Talgarreg
Ceredigion
SA44 4HB

Broken Sleep Books Ltd
Fair View
St Georges Road
Cornwall
PL26 7YH

Missing Person

Nicholas Hogg

Broken Sleep Books

Contents

I

II

III

IV

V

I

You move from now to now, crumpling time up in your hands,
tossing it away. You're your own speeding car. You think
you can get rid of things, and people too—leave them behind.
— Margaret Atwood, *The Blind Assassin*

Missing Person

I was a convict boy who dreamed of running.
No surprise that the men who had
got my attention. It was on a job near Heathrow,

driven out to a verge in a minibus
crammed with my fellow have-nots. We were hefting mulch
around sapling trees, squinting in the gale force

draft from the haulage trucks, when I found the bag.
Like looking at a corpse, the three of us
stood and stared. Big enough to hold a body,

the weight of a life. *You unzip it. No, you.* I pulled slowly,
like defusing a bomb. The payload damp and rife with mould.
We found a bunch of keys. Socks, boots, shorts, and jeans.

And a brand new pair of shoes, which the lad from Stockport took,
along with a watch that had no strap. We rummaged in the pockets
for money. Nothing but a Polaroid

soldier in the wild, smiling for the lens in his camo gear. We studied
his face for clues. Of what, God knows. Then we got back to work.
I'm not sure about the other two, shovelling

shit on minimum wage, but I was jealous. Here was a man
who'd stepped from his skin, scrubbing out a name and starting again.
Dead or alive. I wonder if he hears the traffic

like I still do, rattling a soul from a ribcage. Or how the airport
booms with soaring jets, the wing tips
trimmed with light.

Butlins

There will be a monorail that loops rows of wooden shacks
painted in primary colours. The beach, an agonisingly
shallow slant into the mud brown wash of the North Sea,
will be of no consequence to the enjoyment of the holiday.
This will be provided by the staff in Red Coats,
or pirate costumes, pursued by gangs of kids
including me, my sister, and the two daughters
of my mum's best mate, who is also a divorcee
ditched on a crap estate. We'll ride donkeys
that don't kick, bite, or stink, and the arcade
will offer games with multiple lives and endless credit,
where I'll clock *Paperboy* on a ten pence piece.
And my mother, twirled in a blizzard of light and Babycham,
while I rock my knees like Elvis, won't kiss a man and leave.

Kayak

You could look down into the River Soar
and see thick green reeds
wimpling in the glassy flow. There were bullheads
and sticklebacks, the rumours of a lobster
that was obviously a crayfish. I remember
when Mick Fairlight found an old kayak
rotting in the grass, and we carried it back
to his house on Goodes Lane
where his dad commandeered it, patching up
the holes with gaffer tape, before tying it
to his roof rack. It was a weekday, but he hadn't
worked for months so he had plenty of spare time
to drive us all down to the Gate Hangs Well.
His only real commitment was to fighting
his eldest son in the box room.
Anyway, he might be dead now, I don't know.
What I do recall is how he launched the kayak
from the pub garden, pushing it out into the river
and paddling furiously
as the frame collapsed and the water gushed in.

Longbow

First we'd climb the fence into the garden centre,
a barbed wire castle, before stealing six-foot lengths of cane
and wading through the brook to the College Road bridge,
where we'd set them tight with nylon string
and flex them into bows,
strumming an instrument of violence and war,
once favoured by Stone Age nomads, Japanese horsemen,
and Robin Hood, who wore Lincoln green on ITV.

When the bow was sprung, we fletched arrows with dart flights
and pigeon feathers, before shaving down the points
with penknives – needle-sharp splinter-ends, that could draw
blood from fingertips, or stand proud in the eye of a king.
Then we stalked the woods for rabbits, burying the shaft
deep in a time-travelling Norman, falling from a battlement.
Note the pierced armour as he paddles the air, the flight
like a brooch pinned to his heart.

Pyro

Let's go up to Deville Park and hunt
for spent casings of fireworks from last night.
We can scrape out the powder charge
and mix our own rockets and bangers and terrorise
the estate. Or get your brother
to buy us a box of explosives from the newsagents
near the train track, the one that sells single fags
and Scandia Green. I know you lost your eyebrows
lighting that air bomb, but I'll be more careful
this time, I promise. Come on,
I'm bored of chucking aerosol cans into the fire
and playing that game of chicken where we wait
for them to burst like a shotgun shell.
And there's nothing else to do. Your dad
beats your mother, and mine is a drunk.

Corporal Punishment

We were caught
looting a cupboard. The Head
was alone

at the door, watching us
steal. Tracksuit boys
in a tableau, clutching brand new pens

we could sell to the lads
who tagged. In the film
a biker gang

walk into a bar
owned by the Mafia. The Don
greets the bikers with a smile,

before he locks the door. And the men
appear with bats. Cracking
skulls

and smashing teeth. Our Don, the Head,
had checked the empty corridor,
locked the door,

and smiled. Robbie Culsen
jackknifed over the desk like a broken doll.
When he slapped Richard Purse it sounded

like gunshot. I forget the speech he made
about thieving bastards
as he put his elbow to my throat.

Chameleon

You would believe, watching the way
he strokes the chin of his pet

chameleon, that this soul
knows nothing about torture

or tying a drug dealer to a chair
and leaving him for days.

When a chameleon changes colour
it mimics the surrounding

palette, blending into brick or leaf,
prey or foe. What skin

would you take
on this estate, with that father?

Video Game

Pac-Man was a prophet, Donkey Kong a god.
The arcade was a church, and deliverance from this world
to the next, was a start button. By hopping over barrels,
or eating the dead, I could rise from the ruins of a broken
home in a broken town, and fly a supersonic jet
at the edge of space. My best friend died in a Battlezone.
Another died running with a plumber in a sewer.
I've seen the kingdom, where the golden bird is freed
from her cage, and the air is filled with mutant bats
and ships in flame, and the boss can kill with a fireball.
What I really wanted, beyond a High Score name
on a title screen, was a glitch. A gateway graphic
where the pixel split, and I stepped on through
to the 8-bit plane.

Starring Role

I never auditioned,
but I got the part of TEENAGE RUNAWAY – boy in a park
      camped beneath a slide.
The camera tracks me as I walk
      bedraggled in the rain. I perform
      my own stunts

when I go back home (while he's out)
      and break in
through the kitchen door. You see me collect
books and clothes,
      my last few scraps of money. No lingering shot
      where I gaze at a photo, the happy family

posed in a gilded frame.
Cut to another door opening,
      a smiling face.
I set my bag down in a basic room. All I carry
      is all I own.
      Zoom: count the coins in my palm. Skint,

as I hang around town, a wet bleak street,
      and a kid my age
shopping with his mum. I'm on the road still
when a van crawls by,
      and you wonder what turn
      this film will take.

No. We have a beaming grin. Laughter and chat,
        before a handshake
cut to the very next day, and I'm in the front seat.
We see men in hard hats as the van pulls up.
            Montage: lugging hammers,
            hitting nails, tacking panels.

Then a tea with the lads,
        the ruffle-haired cub. I wander off
from the gang – cue plaintive strings (not too loud)
        as I stand and stare from a new-build shell.
A reviewer may write
        that this is rather mawkish,

the boy at a window
in an empty home. What the critic
has failed to gather, is how the man will carry
        this void
        into every room he walks
        for the rest of his life.

Phobia

We used to play a game called Stuntman,
I explain, when once again I'm called a psychopath
because I don't get scared on fairground rides.
I try to convey that fear
was leaping off the Co-op roof into a skip
filled with cardboard,
and a box of broken tube lights
spiked underneath. Or the act of faith
required when jumping from the canal bridge
into the lock, and not knowing
if a discarded trolley, stolen bike, or the rusted
prong of some lethal trap, was waiting in the deep.

Once you've given in to the dynamics of riding
a motorbike with no helmet
the wrong way up a by-pass,
because it shows the other kids you are fearless
and can't be fucked over without consequence,
then screaming on the log flume at Alton Towers
seems pointless. In a loop on a rail
at a hundred feet
I sit, immune to fright.

One man who had me sussed
was the soldier I met in Goa, talking war
in a beachside bar. I challenged him to a swim
out to some rocky point in the moonless dark,
and he grinned,
turned back to his beer, and dared me
to read him a poem.

II

I heard an airplane passing overhead. I wished I was on it.

— Charles Bukowski, *Ham on Rye*

Northern Lights

My latest escape plan
is to fly over the Pacific Northwest
in a single prop plane that valiantly
battles the polar wind. I'll land
on the gravel bar of a glacial river
and stake claim to a plot of woodland
with a log cabin sturdy enough to keep out
bears and wolves. My axe will tring
in the morning quiet.
There will be treks across meadows of white,
through pine trees ruffled in snow.
Perhaps I'll walk out onto a frozen lake,
listening for that heart-stopping sound
like a steel cable snapping.
But the ice will hold my weight,
and with a gloved hand
I'll wipe it clear so I can look down
and shudder. Then back to the hearth
where I'll read Jack London and Cormac McCarthy,
the Wyoming Stories of Annie Proulx.
Tales about lives
set against the cold, the Arctic night,
on a page that glows by a single bulb,
where the black type is anthracite,
and the words spark fire.

Mariner

A boy drifts out to sea on a cheap blue lilo
bought with his holiday money. His father
told him not to go beyond the harbour wall,
but he had read a book about Captain Cook
as a wanderlust youth on a coal barge bound
for the globe. Although the boy will make it
home, arms burning, more embarrassed
by his trial than scared, he will dream of a ship
from his bedroom. There will be monsters, yes.
And the kraken is awake in the depths of the house
as he dives on the treasure of an atlas, the torch-light
gold on the coast of Peru.

20,000 Leagues Under the Sea

Banging in the dark on a Friday night, the front door
clattered like a battened hatch smashed, before his

drunken wallow up the stairs. As if the street were at sea
and my house a cabin. Confined to my quarters,

I dreamed of waves, I drowned monsters in a foaming storm.
I was Kirk Douglas on the Nautilus, with a knife

between my teeth. The harpoon hero with a dimpled chin,
killing off a giant and saving his crew. But watch

the dead squid's slow descent, how the ink and the blood
entwine. And the unfortunate sailor, still wrapped in his grip.

California

I have not lived in Manchester
with thieves, but I have hitchhiked across the USA
with a knife. The thieves I lived with

were in Leicester, and the yobs I once fought
I escaped, by reading On the Road, buying a ticket
to New York, and standing on the edge

of a highway to Boston, where I slept like a king
on a concrete step. That was the morning
I stole a tourist map, and drew

a matchstick figure with a giant thumb,
the plucky little hitcher with a pilgrim's want
of the mythical West – as if that glittering sea

could save the world. Between the blue oceans
I was chased, caught, robbed, and kissed. There was
the waitress in Chicago, and the drug dealer

in Seattle, who played Van Morrison, and shot
three-pointers in the park while high
on coke. Their faces I forget.

What I do recall is waking in a range of crumpled
peaks, the granite hills wound by wagon trains bearing
God and cholera, perhaps an arrow shaft

broken in two.
And the great wide spangle of light,
the Pacific, where we stopped our car and picked up stones.

Cop Show

You can walk all day in New York.
Live through the crowd of faces
on the move
in a frozen street.

They have that steam,
like a subway
ghost. Sure, I took photos,
but I never captured

the grubby essence. How a rat
gang would stand its ground,
ripping up a hot dog
limb from bun.

Or a beer full of light
at Happy Hour, glowing
like a flare. I once hit the whiskey
with a bonafide cliché,

a drunken
cop who had lost his badge. *I shot
a kid running from a hold up.*
He was looking at the dregs

at the bottom of his glass.
It was him or me.
He lifted up his rye for a toast.
Fuck it, he said. *Fuck it all.*

Gun (With Englishman)

Have you ever held a gun before?
I once fired a revolver, point-blank at Mark Stoneley,
loaded with a roll of paper caps. He cried,
and told his mum, who told my mum. So, *No, not really.*
We drove towards Mexico, through sand dunes
littered with shoes, a rag doll snagged on a barbed wire fence.
He said, *It's not a toy,* and then made me put it together
like a puzzle. Barrel, slide, frame, and the jet-black magazine.
Heavy as the dark in a folding star. Along a dirt track
lined by cholla and scrub, the road signs
peppered with lead, I snapped in the rounds. *Here.* We stopped
by a runnel and a pockmarked fridge, where he pinned up
a target, and showed me how to aim. *Squeeze off the noise,*
he said, pumping out shot. The desert took the sound
and buried it. *Your turn.* I stood as instructed,
bucking on a kick when the gun went BANG, trying to be tough
when the clip was spent. Or so I thought. He took back the Glock
and tutted, holding up a round still left. *They're the ones
that kill.* Without a doubt, the fridge was dead. Holes
in the front door, holes through the rear, bleeding light.
I want to add a detail here, like circling birds, or a dust devil swirl.
But, no. Just a fridge. And a target flayed with a heart
blown out.

Speed Trap

The blue light sparked
A young boy
on hilt, twitchy. We were
was my excuse.

this big
the boy with the ticket.
if you drive a little slower.
slowly, but not slow enough.

doing thirty
They were sitting
sipping ice tea. One of the men
and swore. Watched a hat

paunch. I gave him the book,
embossed on the cover.
the pages
That's Ay-rab writing.

calling in for help.
pulled up.
got out. Thumbs
sharp. *Sir.*

I'm an author.
What's an author?
You did. In your best
like a mystery writer.

in the rear view mirror.
dressed as a cop. Hand
tiny in a landscape. *It's Texas,*
We don't get sky

in England. He liked that,
You'll enjoy the country more
He tipped his hat as I drove away,
We were shot

in the very next town.
with a speed gun
hit the siren. We stopped
walk up with a Big Mac

the golden crown
He studied my photo,
stamped with foreign ports.
He read with concern,

Another car
Another cop
tucked, silver star
What's your job?

The men stared.
I had no answer.
Country Girl drawl. *You know,*
The men nodded. *You write books?*

Yes, sir.
Kind of.
got kidnapped.
That's it. She broke his legs.

He had a notebook
named. We could feature
It's a great novel, I said.
He capped the nib, and paused.

Then he tapped the roof
move along a horse.
for the state line. You raged
hustle. *I have warrants,*

They can lock me up
was a bayou,
in shotgun shacks,
now, high above a river

Like Stephen King?
I read that one about a writer
Misery.
Made him change the ending.

ready. Pen drawn. Characters
in a story of our own.
Have you seen the movie?
I prefer the book.

to let us go. Like a man might
We drove
about the cops, the toll booth
you know.

here. The border
where the outlaws hide
and we were laughing
in a rented car.

Sarajevo Grammar

We walked on a trail where the landmines slept, high upon a hill
above smoke and ruin – where she stopped, and pointed:

> *See the crumpled dome of the bombed-out mosque,*
> *the tramway torched and mangled.*
> *There were books on the breeze when the library*
> *burned, remember, it was on the news.*
> *And you, watching from your sofa.*
> *The parchment charred and fluttered,*
> *falling on the town like thick black snow.*

I also met a vet who talked with glee. Muzzle flash
and missile speed, how a round impacts and stratifies flesh.
From a trigger on a peak you could nullify a life
in a downtown street.

> *Pazite, Snajper!*

Read the handmade sign. Language could protect and save, after all.

So this is why a man, who ran from a shop as the snipers fired
from a barrel in a trench, held a paper to his head like a bullet-proof shield.
A folded daily, filled with horoscopes and football, an abandoned quiz.

He was killing time. Waiting for the day when the MIG flights stopped
and the cafes opened. When the market bustled and the shelling ceased.
He was waiting for a game of chess in the Old Town, thinking out a move
and drinking tea, while another man tuned to a channel from the Hague.

Where a shock of grey hair (like a doomsday swirl of thundercloud smoke)
shook a fist
at words.

Fiji

On my first day in the village
　　　　　　the men dug a fire pit
and filled it with leaves and the cuts of a fat sow
that had been led across a field
　　　　　　and then killed
　　　　　　on a strip of corrugated tin.

This is how we used to cook the priests,
　　　　　　said the Chief.
In 1830 the missionaries docked with books
　　　　　　about God and sin,
　　　　　　how flesh was evil – both to eat and bare.
Last year I jumped down from a truck with a cardboard box

crammed with copies of the National Geographic – glossy features
　　　　　　on lions and space,
　　　　　　the lit cities wired to the dark globe.
There were stories on rain and famine, the machines of war.
How oil wells
　　　　　　burned in a pockmarked desert.

But what the orbiting lens
　　　　　　did not capture
was the tail of the Milky Way
　　　　　　twinkling
　　　　　　in a palm tree
as I walked back stoned from a night of dance

and kava – the peppery soma drunk from wooden bowls,
                or human skulls,
if I believed in the old sots
cackling and slapping their thighs
                when I sipped
                and gritted my teeth.

The magazine also failed to report
on the mornings in a clapboard school
                where children
                sang the teachers into class,
and wrote poems in chalk about parrots, and fish
                drifting in a stream.

There were no photos of the silence when ripe fruit
                dropped from a branch
                and into my hand.
Or how the Chief and I dived on the wreck
of a Chinese trawler
                as sea snakes

                circled above.
By then I was swimming in the Pacific like a local, and I believed
in the fable of truce between men and sharks,
that the world was a myth
                on a printed page.
                A Technicolor epic in smoke and flame.

Calais Pier

Critics compared his use of paint to blots, batter, pea soup, smoke, a mix of soap and chalk, and the veins on a marble slab. The painting was unsold and remained in Turner's possession.'

— The National Gallery

In the eggshell blue above Venice, in the ice cream cloud on a park in France,
the storm abates. Even in an English meadow, where the gentry and a hound
stand puffed and proud, the weather has held – see the sugar baron
posed with a pheasant and a gun. But on through the gilded rooms,
the centuries styled in shadow and light, the gold in the straw at Lady Jane's
death, and how the upturned axe, whetted to an edge near diamond sharp,
pierces the gloom. Before the Turner with a storm now trapped in a frame,
the turbulent world at war with the sea. Note: the poor souls doomed
on a Calais pier, piling into boats that bump and jostle, the white wave flare
and the rolled up sail, the wooden hull swamped and the oarlock rattle.
And how the artist works in thick grey paint, cutting up the Channel in a squall.
What colour would you mix for a dinghy made of rubber? The life raft
ditched on a beach in Kent? It's only a brush stroke, you tell yourself, the faces
lit by panic and fear.

July

In a classroom on Edgware Road,
        as the boys with bombs
catch London trains, I draw the layout of a Crown Court,
        representing justice
with a red marker pen. The students compete with each other
on spelling checks
and survival stories. There is the man who walked from Kabul
        to France

because the Taliban found his Bee Gees tape. A jumped up teen
smashed the *Best of* into pieces,
        while another held a gun
        to his hairless chin, and promised
        to kill him
if he didn't grow a beard. When I ask if he walked all the way
he tells me that he was born in the mountains.
Although his friend

did die by the road
in Hungary. Near Dieppe he climbed into a lorry
filled with tomatoes, and only got out when he heard
        English voices.
The Lebanese tailor, a dapper dressed gent in a three-piece suit,
        likes to brag about the burning car
that landed on his roof. Now the fierce old Somali woman tuts.
        She has scars on her hands

and face. Her house was pierced by an RPG,
unexploded, hissing on the floor like a cornered bird.
        The Congolese giant

nods. He hid in the woods and held his breath, watching
while his neighbours walked through the trees
             with machetes. And the Palestinian
artist, tortured by men who put a hole in his kidney
             with a hand drill.

But I really must stop the students here. We can't get started on
the Eritrean woman
             sold as a child bride, and how she crossed
the border in a bouncing truck, wearing only
             her wedding dress.
And certainly not the Kosovan soldier, a real talker,
the one who met Tony Blair on a runway. No. Not today.
             We have a test.

Hitchhiker

Thumb out to the flow of traffic, and hoping not
to get robbed, mugged, or murdered.
But also a lift. I step into cars, vans, and trucks. I once rode a rocket
fired down the M1 – a Ford Cosworth, stolen – like a sonic boom jet
in the outside lane.

I meet Samaritans and chancers.
One man will explain Islam, another will talk about
fucking lorry drivers. A fashion designer, who picks me up
from a garage forecourt, will give me a mint
while her dog growls from the back seat.

On a roundabout near Bedford,
another hitcher waits. He wears a trench coat, and boots
once worn by a paratrooper. He also has a crucifix
tattooed on his forehead, just below his mohican. We say hello.
He's going to a party in Leeds. I'm going to Leicester, to see my sister.

No one picks him up. No one picks me up.
Occasionally, I think about him. Punk Jesus on a pilgrimage.
More often I think about the teacher who cried
recalling a holiday to Scotland
with his dying son,

and how they took a row boat onto a loch
so thick with mist
that the known world shrank to a bubble of white.
Borne along the highway in a Vauxhall Cavalier, I saw,
through his eyes,

how the mist would clear and a castle
reveal, the unexpected ramparts sealed with moss.
And then the boy in the boat
leaping ashore. Up and over the broken stone,
joyous. A prince in a fable with a palace of his own.

Hanuman

At the top of the hill
is a white-washed temple
as bright as snow.
Sitting on a rock
like an outcast priest
is a monkey.
The wind ruffles his fur,
and he considers the peaks,
the light on the river.
How a lone hawk
rides the breeze.
And he shuns the tourist
who sits on a wall and waits,
catching his breath.
While monkey
watches the world
I see the shadow of a flag,
rippling.
It swims in the sun
like a soul of fish
trapped
when the seas dried up.
Monkey turns
and looks me in the eye,
opens his mouth to speak.
I expect wisdom.
Edicts on time and space,
the nature of god.
But he is older than words,

the grammar of talk,
and he beats his chest and screams.
The jester with a fang-tooth grin,
throwing his shit
off the side of a mountain.

Haiku

For a week in Tokyo
I ate nothing
except the free samples
given out at fancy department stores.

Octopus legs and squid,
the sweet bean cakes and strong green tea,
some heat in my bones.
Then I'd walk home in the neon frost,

still hungry,
and think about Bashō on the road near Fuji,
considering the wind and the rain,
how the withered grass shimmers

at the coming spring.
One time he wished
for the clothes of a tattered scarecrow.
Another night so cold

that the rice jar cracked.
Well, in my cheap small room,
where the ice will form and the mould
will thrive, I heard the pot break.

And then Bashō rise,
picking up his cane and putting on his robe,
counting out the sounds
while he set them on the page.

Vegas

The mirage is wired by a billion volts,
hapless dreams, hot dog meals, and the ghost of Elvis,
singing down the sun
over palm trees and pyramids, showgirls and drunks.

You can sip a soap-like shot
in a deafening bar. Watch a stag-do gang
roam the mall and the Strip,
wasted in neon, clinging to their cups of flat warm beer.

What happens in Vegas, stays in Vegas.
Especially your money.
Strolling the indoor walkways, between slot machines
and card games,

where the white ball rattles in a turning wheel,
and the chumps (like us) fly across the world to win
or lose
the price of a house on the colour of a square,

the novelty of Hell wears thin. But after five
piss-weak margaritas, you should stand on the roof
of a cheap hotel
and squint – you can see stars, high above the desert plain.

III

If you wish to make an apple pie from scratch,
you must first invent the universe.

— Carl Sagan, *Cosmos*

UFO

With my ear to the stars, I listen. This is my job
in the future, when the fires burn out.
In a radar post on a South Sea peak,
a great white bowl on a lush green isle.
The measured technician, checking numbers. I work
for the wonder of what is coming – the alien chatter
from a distant rock. My love
will wear a lab coat, with a red pen clipped
to a starched top pocket. She's adept at everything
I'm not, and when I talk about the light
that zagged across the dark on an outback night,
she'll raise an eyebrow,
and stop. She'll quiz me on the facts,
the fraying of time and recall. *We were stone cold sober.*
So she'll ask about my witness, an Aussie called Bruce.
We both saw the white orb zap across the sky.
She'll ask about velocity, the distance from Earth.
And I'll do the best I can, the plain truth.
Nothing could survive that speed, the G-force turn.
She'll nod, sigh, take out her pen, and jot down a word.
Then she'll lift up her glasses, and stare,
gaze like a lens on a microscope. *What do you want?*
She'll snap, as the radio waves come washing off the void.

Meteor

The stars are like stones
      on jet black velour,
            and the mountains mirror on the sparkled lake.

You can see the high peaks
      smoke with windblown snow,
            as if the crag burned ice at the boundary of space.

The same peaks
      lit by an atom splitting – the photon
         beamed from an alien pyre.

As you drive,
      head craned to the sky,
         to the galaxy of fire that shines this road,

a streak of gold
      unzips the night – a bright long banner of blazing ore,
         criss-crossing planets and moons,

Saturn and Mars,
      a black hole warped in flame and time, to fizzle out here
         like glitter.

We stop the car and gaze.
      Nothing but the image that prints in a blink.
         So you turn the key

and pull away,
   talk about ships and little green men.
     Tunnels, bored through the dark,

and starred with the watts of electric tubes,
   flash and pass.
     We're cramped in the compact,

yet feeling vast.
   Thrilled with the hope of rocks in the void
    still chanced with life.

Interstellar

She tells me the whole universe
has to exist
for this moment
to exist – on a bus into town, where no one
knows her name. *One stray atom*, she explains,
burst from a fissure on a moon
like Titan, could've rocked her fate.
She opens her tin and pinches tobacco, the lurid
buds of green. *You wouldn't have been born*, she says,
crumbling the dope. *And I could've been
a rocket scientist*. She licks the paper and seals the roll.
I wouldn't be on this fucking bus for a start,
she says, looking for a lighter to fire up her joint.
You ain't got a quid have you mate?

Diz

No one told me it was the good old days
when we woke at dawn
and drove out to quarries in battered cars.

We saw the universe swirl and gather in tar
when we turned up for work
from a night out tripping. And what a vision

in the wheat
when it caught on the wind, rippled in a gust
like an ocean gold and blessed

with sun. So what about the cosmos now?
What do you see, Jim? What colour was the dark
when they laid you on the ward?

When we came to nurse you,
bearing gifts of word and touch. When your heart
stopped beating.

Did you feel my hand in yours? I cried about the light
from a dying star. How the heat could fade
in a cooling palm.

The White Dot

I once saw Jesus Christ
in a crop circle,
or at least a man who looked like him,
naked in the middle of a field,
stripped to the sky
and calling for *The Light*.

Like on Christmas Day in 1996,
when I chopped a TV set
clean in half
with a long-handled axe,
and saw the white dot split
like an atom in the sun.

Astronauts

Photographing the nature of bark,
she is an inch from tree.

Everyone else is walking home
and silent en masse – a river of monks

true to their vows. But she is stilled
in the slant of day, and pilots

a lens in orbit. I make my eyes hers,
and see a canyon scroll from a satellite

view, the sun pooled in grooves
where the moss grows

green on a fluted land. And we are
weightless and tiny

on an alien moon, the fast stars
falling like electric snow.

Alien Sex Guide

Driving through San Diego
with an old hippy, hawking books to stores
that sold incense and crystals. Books

with pentagram covers and pictures of angels
in normal clothes, who also had wings,
and a halo. Neither I nor the hippy

had read Witches on Mars, or the hardback
copy of Ghosts in Love. He drove the car
and I held the box. A Summer In Heaven

got fifty bucks, and what we didn't sell
we left on the sidewalk, blowing the cash
on tacos and beer.

High on tequila,
we raised a shot to the Alien Sex Guide,
toasting the author and his noble research.

Fosse Way

Bumping my head against the stars, it seems, as I walk to Nottingham
on Christmas Eve, and then Christmas Day, with the A46 deserted,
save for the ghosts of Roman gods and Saxon slaves, buried
in a thoroughfare dug and barrowed so a drunken youth
can stagger on home. And the guiding light like a beacon, or a sign,
for a Three King jolly. If, that is, Jesus II was a Little Chef baby,
and Balthazar sat with a hot figgy pudding in a faux leather booth.
Still, instead of a stable we have a budget hotel. And the innkeeper
wrecked or sleeping. So I hammer on the glass till it shatters and breaks.
Wait there while I call the police, he says, running to a phone
by a plastic tree. I hide in a ditch for a while, and watch my white breath
smoke on a distant sun. Then I walk North, and the road
sparkles with frost. All your diamond cliches, crushed beneath my boots.
I've travelled this road a thousand times, and never seen the sky this close.

Jupiter

You get a moment,
sometimes, to consider the space
between planets. I open the window
while taking a bath, floating in the clear night sky
with Jupiter. Naked,
the two of us
in orbit.

Mowde Bush Stone

Take the gravel track out past the tumbledown farm
where time is folding in on itself, as if the unlikely

beginnings of a black hole crumpling space
through an old slate roof, avoiding the dead end lane

where doggers and smokers hide from the world with weed
or sex, and then climb the padlocked gate rusted

fast to a concrete post, you'll see a six-foot stone
in the corner of a meadow. This is not the polished monolith

humming with an alien missive. It's a lump of rock
in a deep green field, given meaning by druids and witches,

hippies and frauds, and once worshipped by Victorian mystics
who may have also picked the liberty cap mushrooms

on the Saxon ridge. I like to think, when the psilocybin hit,
that they lay for a while with the flowers and the sky,

watching bees track pollen from petal to petal,
before the universe wall gave way.

IV

I looked out on the throw outside of my window
Outside there wasn't anything nice to see
I wanted things to smell, like meadows, not like hell
Dying dandelions and bumble bees

— Sleaford Mods (feat. Billy Nomates), *Mork N Mindy*

In Bloom

Here come the faceless men, scything at the bush
with two-stroke saws, levelling shrub with a chain link

fired by an ancient trunk. I don't hate the blokes
hacking with the petrol teeth, unlike my cat,

who growls at the digger from an open door,
but I do wonder about the sapphire Pacific

in which I once swam, diving on a reef
where an octopus watched from a fairy tale lair.

Besides, I've done this before,
razing flowers for money.

> When I was a small boy,
> working any job a man would give me,
> I cut the weeds around graves
> one summer, strimming in fear of a pale hand
> pushing up the loam. We bought sweets
> with the pittance. We rode into town, queuing
> for a burger and Coke at the new McDonald's.
> We thought the future would be made
> with chrome and flying cars.
> There would be robots.

Not workmen charged with the vandal
murder of an overgrown plot where the foxes live.

So I walked to the pub, where the sunlight beamed
through a campus dorm, glowing in the empty rooms.

Snowdrops pierced the dark green lawn, and daffodils
could be purchased at Tesco, along with luminous

heather, and plastic grass. By the time I got home
the cat was asleep on the bed, and the men

had finished for the night, after a hard and violent
crime. Without ever travelling to Mars

they have made the yard look like Mars. Instead of aliens
tonight the fox cubs yip and yelp

like tortured souls. For seven long weeks we listen
and watch. Before the bare brown patch

is a miracle. From a dustbowl planet to a verdant
bloom, we see the earth reborn. The rain-shine-rain

has erupted flowers and banks of nettles. The paratroop
seeds have dropped in waves, and the sycamore trees

will stand their ground. The dead stalks rise
from the wreckage of themselves, and the fox cubs,

who curled on the dirt with paws as pillows, pounce
and play. We can take some comfort, now. For all men go,

eventually. Back to the atoms in well-turned soil, to the rocks
that flourish in the dark of space. We are the sun

that yearns through leaf and stem, the amber
in a fossil on an ocean floor.

Stoney Cove

From the mock deck pub
I watch. Bubbles pop and fizz. Frogmen emerge,
dripping, alien. Divers
flood the quarry at weekends, descending
on the objects sunk for their training: helicopter, bus, aircraft, car.
The tugboat *Defiant* and the ancient tree. They practice
for the world submerged
in fathoms of brine and glacial melt,
the children of carbon, to see how we used to live.

Rain

Fizzing in the trees, and the wet leaves
keen with light, what little there is, fuzzy

in the cloud. You forget what keeps this Wednesday
whole, the sphere of fire. Before the break of star

on a golden field, like a warning spark on a whetted
blade, where the sun will burr and sharpen.

It's good to feel the cut, sometimes, to know
the world is true.

Hail

The air is filling with ice.
Alone, I watch the clouds
swirl from the west

like drops of ink in a glass of water.
Before hailstones the size of pearls
dance off cars and trucks.

Yesterday you were here,
and we put cream on our noses
and drove to LA in the sun.

Now you're gone,
and the oranges bruise and windows
crack, broken by sky.

The woman on the hill
will later tell me that this was nothing.
That a week after a storm

had brought down power lines
she found a hailstone under a bush,
still the size of a golf ball.

Whiteout

We thought they were hulks of cloud
in the morning dark, not moving.

Just scissor-cut shapes with a shaking hand,
looming over breakfast. Then the sun

hit the peaks
and the orange snow, the fierce black crags.

We padded up in coats
and hiked through the firs, a petrified

forest in a sugar-brushed glaze.
Hansel and Gretel in goggles and boots,

looking for the lift that rose like a spell.
The magic seat climbing into mist

and fog, where there was nothing
but you.

Dorothy

With her little dog woofing at the woman
on a broom, and a house in flight on a thunderhead
twist of Kansas dirt, I'm Dorothy in spirit
in a campsite storm.

And if the world is left when I wake here
tomorrow, and the caravan has held
to a windblown field
where the stars unhinge from a cosmic wall,

I want the ruby red shoes
and a yellow brick road, not the deckchair wreckage
in a tree by the gate, clanging on a post
like a doom-chime bell.

I want the Technicolor walk
in the opioid dell, the little blue river
in a plastic town where the munchkins chuckle
with a merry old witch. Put me in Oz

while the news is on, where the Taliban trend
and the Red Woods burn. I'll see a bat-winged
chimp and have no fear, leaning on
a friend of gleaming tin.

Leave the wizard alone, let him draw the curtain
and keep on working. He's busy with sky
and puffs of cloud. The polychromic
burst of curving light.

Buttercup

Tearing up the sky
might end. When your

with a searing jet,
in your tended yard.

but water your flowers.
that stagger and bumble

As the new machines
and the clever men

and roar: *I am become*
The buttercup yellow

with sound, is how the Earth
sternum thrums

shuddering bone
What can you do

And speak to the bees
as the war goes on.

arrive in secret hangers,
rip back seals

Death, the destroyer of worlds.
on a broken wall.

Obsidian

The black mirror of rock
I found on a hill, prized by the Maori and atom-sharp,
buried by a cage of bones too big, thankfully, to be human,

has vanished. I was chopping back vines for a forest path,
when the dark gold gleamed from the kauri roots.
Like a lump of space

still pierced with stars. Lightly, I'd run the blade
across my palm, to know the hunter who stalked these trees
for the giant, wingless birds,

that roamed above the bay near Whangamatā,
where the sea-smoothed glass had once washed ashore,
whetted to an edge that cut through flesh.

I was at the airport when I last rolled it around in my hand.
So when I read now that the shards of *Tuhua* used to kill a moa
were dropped on the ground

where the bird had died,
and never to be touched again, I wonder what credence
there is to a curse. The black stone missing as I board the plane.

Drone

On a Cornish shore by a glimmering sea, with the beach and the rock
deserted, left to the whelks and the oarweed kelp, we send up a drone
to know we exist. A bird's-eye view from a God-high lens, a self
composed on a HD screen. See the coastline scroll and the megabyte
surf, the Atlantic roll in crystal vision. An airborne code, we're digital
in flight, skimming to the west on pixel wings, the carbon feathers
that whirr and buzz, whizzing to the coves and worrying fish,
the one lone gull who squawks, and dives. Yes, we're in control
here, master of the craft with livestream shots of sunken ships
and eroding cliffs, the shadow of a seal like a mermaid swimming.
But what did the siren sing? When it rounded the bay and kept on going,
ignoring the call to come back home. Only when the drone
needed us, when the power level dropped and the charge ran down,
did it return. Packed in a box like a body in a coffin. Still breathing, waiting.

Quiddity

Jon is walking on water.
Submerged by only an inch of sea,
the sandbank is a mile out and performs miracles.

At low tide it can surface
like a tan-back whale or a mythical island,
a seam of floating gold.

His aim is nowhere, and progress is made.
Quick steps through a melting mirror,
a self emptied and strange.

And I too am here and happy.
Happy to watch waves unspool like cotton
on a loom, to be simple

in the beauty of distance, the fabric of sky.
As if this one white thread of cirrus
had been spun from surf and tide.

Paradise Lost

By summer he worked
on the roads. Digging holes,
filling holes. Winter

he flew to India and filled his stomach
with balloons of coke
for the flight back. He had a photo

he kept in his overalls pocket.
With a woman on a beach
in Goa. She wore a silk sarong

wrapped around her waist,
and nothing else. He would get stoned
on the Stop-Go board,

and stare at the picture,
while the cars in the queue
would honk and rev.

V

I too have been in the underworld, as was Odysseus,
and I will often be there again.

— Friedrich Nietzsche, *Human, All Too Human*

Archway

I've seen the dead rise from Archway Station, stunned
at the rain on the road, the pigeons and the people.
The silent, powered bikes, that coast up the hill
past a phone box shot with weeds, like a hothouse
flower gone rogue. I've seen the world without us,
where the walls come draped in velvet moss,
and the tanks have turrets infused with rust, tracks
to the sky like a beetle, flipped on its back and burned.
I've been a body on a crossing in a Tokyo street,
running from a shop when the earthquake rocked
and rolled. A neon god, watching, while I joined in
the crowd, crushed and lost. Yet here we are, again.
Sunday morning. The coffee gone cold and the book
still closed. Waiting for the lights to change, a sign.

Concerto

He'll go down the canal and get plastered
on a Sunday, knocking back a bottle of bootleg vodka
that looks like water and tastes like thinners.
For the first hour he'll be comprehensible, and talk with pride
about when he used to work at Imperial Typewriters,
and drank pints of mild in smokey pubs, but only on a Friday.
He'll tell you about the strike in '74, and the picket line of saris
screaming at the police. And from the way he talks,
and looks into the depth of the lock,
or at the bottom of the plastic cup that his mate, Mukesh,
brings along in a battered carrier bag,
you'd think he had sight into sunken worlds.
But after half a bottle the stories become fables,
or lies, depending on how you define fairy tales of alcohol
and loss. He'll tell you that he once rescued a woman
and child
from a burning house in Braunstone, and that the worst thing
he ever did was to sprint across six lanes of a motorway
just to prove he wasn't afraid.
Still, what I want to walk away with today,
along the towpath speckled with leaves,
is how he used to solder the typefaces onto the key levers,
and that he would test the strength and accuracy of his weld
by tapping out each letter against the platen,
only signing off his work on a certain, perfect note.

Tupperware

I've slept in squats with mice, and in rooms with rats,
but not among the birds and the bats in a Camden bridge.
Like the two men curled in a thin grey rag,

backed in the shadows and hiding.
They were lovers from a state where touch
is crime. Where a man can be lynched by a righteous mob,

dragged from his bed, and thrown off a roof. For a week
I made extra sandwiches, and took them cake, neatly packed
in designer Tupperware. I collected the boxes empty,

and returned them full the following day. The men were polite
and shy, shaving in the mirror of a dented can. I watched
a blade glide and cut away stubble, sliding over jaw

and vandalized skin. We chatted about
the weather, the ducks that bobbed on the slow green flow.
And then visas, and fire. How the soft flesh burns,

growing into scars like a poisoned bloom. Until one visit
when the men had gone. I put the wholemeal rounds
on the upturned brick, and rode back

the next morning. The Tupperware was neatly stacked.
With each box clipped so firmly to the other,
they could never be prised apart.

Folklore

If you sit in silence
on a cold afternoon, and see the very first
snowflake

fall and settle on the one bare tree,
you might well believe
that a soul can jump from a woman to a fox.

We went back to her tiny apartment.
She heated up a stew that steamed up the glass.
Each pane was a canvas

pressed in neon. In a room of tatami
she would roll out the bed. A woman of the moon
with skin that glowed

like a white flower burning in a darkened wood.
A fable in the city
come true. The fairy tale glade in a Tokyo

forest of tower block gods with concrete mouths.
Where a man might wander
and vanish.

Erebus and Terror

Can bones – skeleton bones – be seen there now when snow
& ice are gone? Ans. She thinks not for it is so muddy there
& the mud soft that they have all sunk down into it — she
continues one man's body when found by the Inuits flesh all
on & not mutilated except the hands sawed off at the wrists
– the rest a great many had their flesh cut off as if some one
or others had cut it off to eat.

> — Charles Francis Hall notebook, May 14, 1869.
> (Hall interviewed Nunavut native, Eveeshuk,
> while on an Arctic expedition to discover the
> fates of HMS Erebus, HMS Terror, and their
> missing crew.)

***

After signing up drunk with an X for a name,
on the promise of rum and scurvy, and the whitecap peak

where you prayed to the Lord that a soul might drown
and float to the light from a godless deep,

this scrabble of land is The End. I wonder what plans you'd made
in a year of Dickens. Workhouse, gaol, and the hangman's noose.

Or a South Sea port with a pagan love, where a wife could be bought
for a pried out nail. Now you're praying for a lump of seal.

Staring at a ration in a lead-lined can, and the storm cloud
bruise on your poisoned skin. Forget about the scars

that decorate your spine, the yelp of shame when the first lash
cut – that cat o' nine weal is dust on the wind. Your bones,

the vertebrae knobbles like pebbles on a beach, will mingle and turn
with the local stone. Your blood will freeze and kaleidoscope ice.

Parts of you, the soft meat dressed with a boarding knife,
will be chewed and swallowed by the starveling crew.

Who in turn will be served as a final meal. Face it, your captain
has gone. And a ship with china on varnished shelves will sink

to the dark of a barnacled grave. But fear not. In the surgeon's tent
is a bottle in a case, a fortified mix of cocoa wine. Drink to the cold

and the beauty of tundra, to the Inuit lore that carries this tale.
You're dead, boy, a *qallunaat* ghost on a frozen shore.

Trespass

The fire core glows like a hole in the earth, and our faces
hang like masks, pinned to the dark. We're fugitives,
hiding out for a night in the New Forest. Hiding out
from the rangers and the locals, the hikers and the Crown,
the farmer with a rifle primed and cocked for the innocent
soul without crime or tent, just sitting by the coals
and drinking, mindful of the beasts that surface in the light.
They nose at the edge of scent and vision, pulse and fear,
twitching, when the ragged sparks flurry and the branches
crack. They keep a sentry in the trees who whinnies and neighs.
No warning of the police who greet us in the morning,
the white wagon churning on the wet mud track. When the van
door slams, a young colt skitters, biting at the air. The horses
watch while the officers write. Names and dates. No Fixed Abode.

The Sirens of Camden

One night drunk in another century, I met a girl
who took me home. She lived in a house with women

who sang by candlelight. Pillars of wax lay pooled on the floor
like bags of skin, and the shadows on the wall

had multiplied, as if each woman were attended
by a sister of the underworld. There were other men there, too,

swept to the cove from pubs and clubs, the indie-hole dives
where rock bands formed. When the women sang,

and called upon the dead to eat the living,
we could have left, hailed down a cab, and fled.

But what we really wanted, the boys in a room
like sailors at sea, was a sacrifice. To be summoned

from our clothes by a priestess
high on voice and wine. Stripped to the quick

by a polyphonic spell of sex and song,
we could swim to the ship in the morning, shorn of soul.

The First Human to Wear Gold

Out by the river, picking over driftwood
bleached like bone. Or digging in the earth
      for a succulent root,
          when the light

once forged in an ancient star
is found. Nugget of fire from a neutron
      bomb so bright
          that the sky still burns.

Now rolled in a palm. Set beside a mammoth
tusk carved and worn as a pagan charm,
      the pendant
          gleams. Gold

in the heat of a dying
flame, how the eyes of a hunter will circle
      at dusk, hacking at meat
          and honing blade,

waiting on sleep. When the lump of sun
will glow. Yellow
      in the hollow
          of a naked throat.

Royalty

In the alleyways walled by brick and fence,
spike and barb, where the backyard guards
are the pictures of dogs
on padlocked doors, another pleb falls.

Among the shining
spines of bloodied needles, the burnt-out
wreck of a moped – torched and dumped
like a mob-hit corpse – the broken glass

has caught the sun. What once
was a bottle of brandy
crunched underfoot, where the dealers prowl
like starving cats, is now a glitter of gems

and precious. And if you're high enough,
drunk, or determined to view the world
through a lens of beauty
or ignorance, note the emerald weeds

where the squatters won't live,
growing on the slate of a derelict house.
This is the wrong end of town.
A mile from the gate where Richard III

was slung
naked on a horse and speared in the buttocks
to be sure that he was dead,
there are junkies curled like the car park king.

Jackpot

Fear the dog running on a flat-roof pub,
barking at the thugs and the drunks, the two blokes
flogging bacon

lifted from Aldi. The best Christmas I ever had
in that dump
was before the landlord put a Bullmastiff up there.

Tony had lost our last twenty quid
on a game of pool, and it was like the angel Gabriel
had appeared

when a thief
with a box of Bell's whisky
came tinkling through the door. You could see the light

on his face beamed down by God.
It was either that or the fruit machine,
paying out and glowing.

Gazza

I never planned to write a poem
about England's greatest ever footballer
absolutely wrecked
in Leicester Market,
buying King Size Rizla from a head stall.
But here we are, on a hot day in June,
the anonymous drunk in stonewash denim,
cutting through the crowd with a ball at his feet,
in my mind, at least, like the goal that he scored
when he shot down the Scots
with a volley in the sun. All around the ground
you could hear his name. From a dentist's chair
to the fabled tunnel, to a crap city pub
where the men measure time by an emptied pint.
Paul, mate. Paul. Can I get you a taxi?
The boy who cried in Turin. The knockabout clown
with a gift from God, washed in booze
and lost. *I'm grand, man. Grand.*
He patted my back and grabbed my arm,
brushing off a tackle. I left him in the bar
with a pocketful of cash, chucking notes at the staff
like snow.

Fantasy

Love the reader in a pub, lost
in a book. A paperback

filled with the elves at war
in a land

where a crystal tower
is a palace under siege

by a dragon
whose days are numbered.

I never read such books, usually,
but in a dead town

drunk as a tonic for the pain,
setting off merry with a legion

called by clinking sword
and decorous shield, the flagons of ale

that make one brave,
has some appeal. Before the reader

in a corner has sunk
his pint, the beast will stir and burn.

And the man at the bar
will drink, quenching fire.

Reading Heaney

In a bar
where the lads watch footy
on a phone. The all-new mob
with fake Armani and guns at home.
Your best friend's ex
saw a man

       hacked to pieces

by the old City ground. How the gang
cleared away the meat
before the police arrived.

       No body.
       No name.
       No crime.

Close your eyes. Close
the award-winning book, and ride
past the leisure centre
risen from the ruin of a redbrick pub.
What happened

       to the band of misfit
       drunks

you met one Christmas Day. You were bound
by family discord. Throwing down beer
like the world

was on fire, and the only way
to save it

was to drown it
in hops. Have you kept in touch
with Gary from Castlebar.
How exotic

to meet a man
who punched

like a bear
and read
like a poet. Some of the first lines
you ever wrote
found his voice. *Seamus*

who?
You'll find out.

He had a ghost on his shoulder,
Gary. Sitting on a boat
near Carrowmore Beach, when a tow line
snapped

and spat.
What friend can watch

as another must go. The light on the wharf
too late.

This grief he gave
his all,

when a dealer in a club
kicked off. In the flurry of glass
and fountain blood,
he spoke Gaelic.

Popping
fist

and vowel. I owed him
for a poem, and threw a cheap
shot, before the doorman
culled us both.
That night

has gone. A ribbon
of film.

What have I left
but words.

Phoenix

In from a long day
shovelling stone. Bruised, cut, sore.
Covered in flecks of thick black tar. When the poet
walks in. She reads to a room

half-filled with chairs.
Lines about leopards. *The otherworld ice* on a frozen tree.
Then there is the verse
that she sang.

A voice full of birds
in the heady summer air. My next shift starts at dawn.
A sleepless night of tropical
dream, before the first clean

slice of gravel, the crunch
and swing. The ring-a-ding scatter on the swirling
dark. I rise up
with the heat of melting tar,

dizzy in a murmur of starling
words. When the bitumen clags
and binds
on steel, you must wet them in diesel

and set them on fire. Hoisting up the shovels
like flaming wings. Driver
beware: the avian pyre on the A46, the navvy poet
feathered like a burning sun.

Acknowledgements

Huge thanks to the editors and journals in which some of these poems first appeared: *Ambit, Anthropocene, Bad Lilies, bath magg, Blizzard Football Quarterly, Finished Creatures, Friday Poem, Interpreter's House, London Magazine, Magma, New European, North, Poetry Birmingham, Poetry London, Shooter Literary Magazine, Southword, Stand,* and *Under the Radar.*

Longbow was first broadcast in 2022 on the Robin Hood episode of *The Rest is History.*

Concerto won the 2021 Gregory O'Donoghue International Poetry Prize and *Missing Person* won the 2023 Liverpool Poetry Prize. *Calais Pier* was runner up in the Wells Festival of Literature Open Poetry Competition, and *Tupperware* in the Freedom From Torture Open Poetry Competition. Other poems here were finalists in the Bedford Poetry Prize, Fish Poetry Prize, and the Troubadour International Poetry Prize.

Phoenix quotes from the Ruth Padel poem, *Icicles Round a Tree in Dumfriesshire.*

I am especially grateful for support from the Society of Authors, Charles Cumming at the Siobhan Loughran Memorial Scholarship, and an Art Omi Writers Residency award.

Special thanks must also go to early manuscript editors, Will Burns, and Richard Beard, whose encouragement and expertise was vital in preparing *Missing Person.* And loving gratitude forever to dressmaker extraordinaire, Melanie James, for drumming the backbeat to the writing of this book.

Finally my heartfelt appreciation to the dynamo that is Aaron Kent at Broken Sleep Books, whose enthusiasm to see a collection spurred me into action.

LAY OUT YOUR UNREST